HOW THINGS
WORK
EVERYDAY MACHINES
Coloring Book

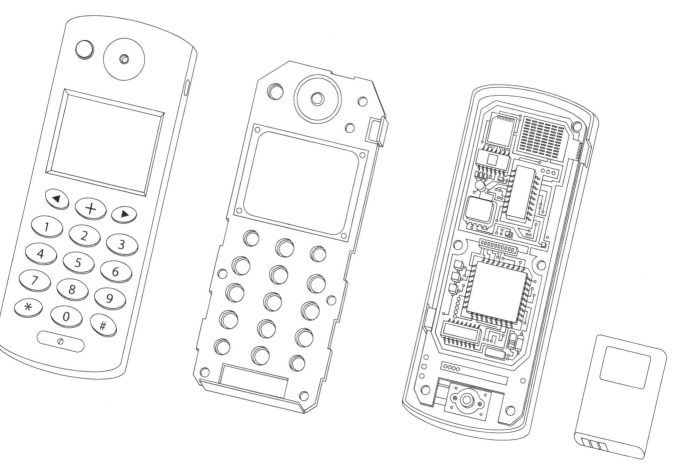

Scott MacNeill

DOVER PUBLICATIONS, INC.
Mineola, New York

Bibliographical Note

How Things Work: Everyday Machines Coloring Book is a new work,
first published by Dover Publications, Inc., in 2013.

International Standard Book Number

ISBN-13: 978-0-486-49220-9
ISBN-10: 0-486-49220-6

Manufactured in the United States by LSC Communications
49220603   2017
www.doverpublications.com

COFFEEMAKER

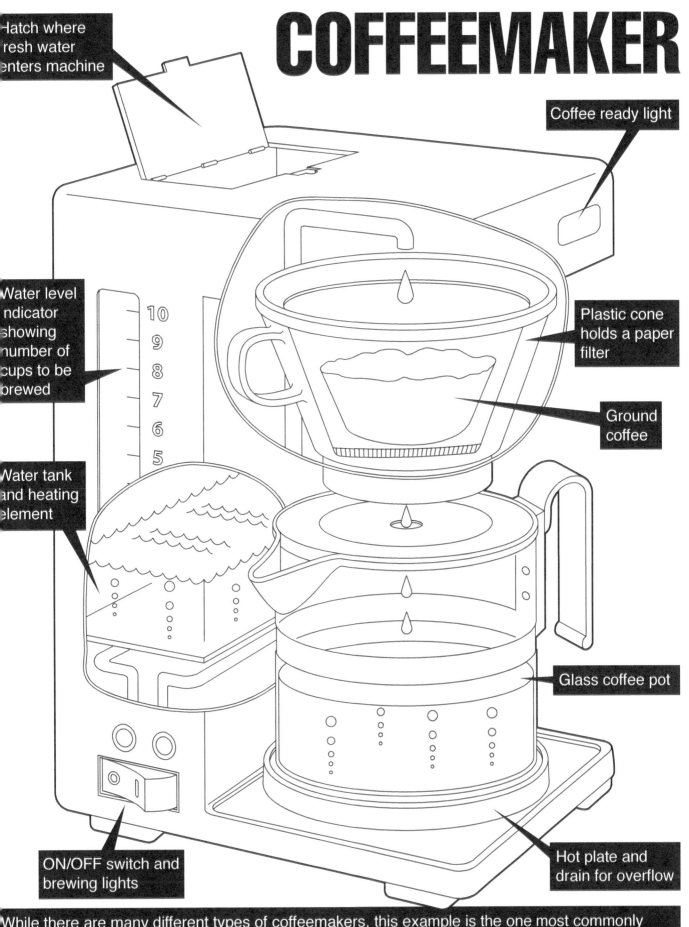

Hatch where fresh water enters machine

Coffee ready light

Water level indicator showing number of cups to be brewed

Plastic cone holds a paper filter

Water tank and heating element

Ground coffee

Glass coffee pot

ON/OFF switch and brewing lights

Hot plate and drain for overflow

While there are many different types of coffeemakers, this example is the one most commonly found brewing up an American family's morning "Cup of Joe."

AMPLIFIER

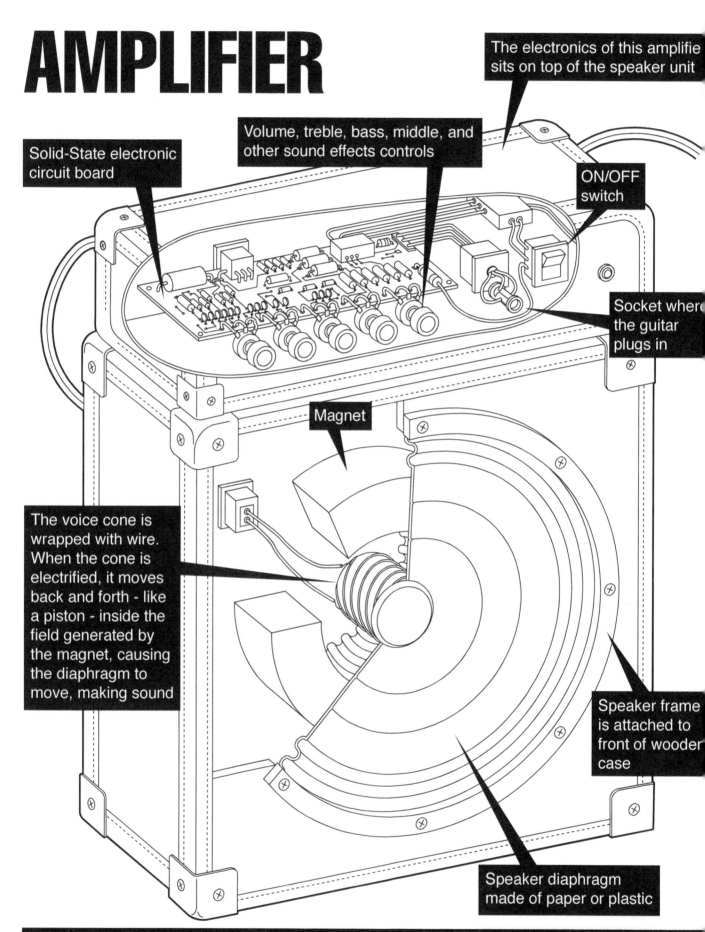

The electronics of this amplifier sits on top of the speaker unit

Volume, treble, bass, middle, and other sound effects controls

Solid-State electronic circuit board

ON/OFF switch

Socket where the guitar plugs in

Magnet

The voice cone is wrapped with wire. When the cone is electrified, it moves back and forth - like a piston - inside the field generated by the magnet, causing the diaphragm to move, making sound

Speaker frame is attached to front of wooden case

Speaker diaphragm made of paper or plastic

Crank it up to 11! Here is a Half-Stack music amplifier as used by musicians to produce sound from an electric or acoustic guitar at volumes impossible without this electronic sound booster.

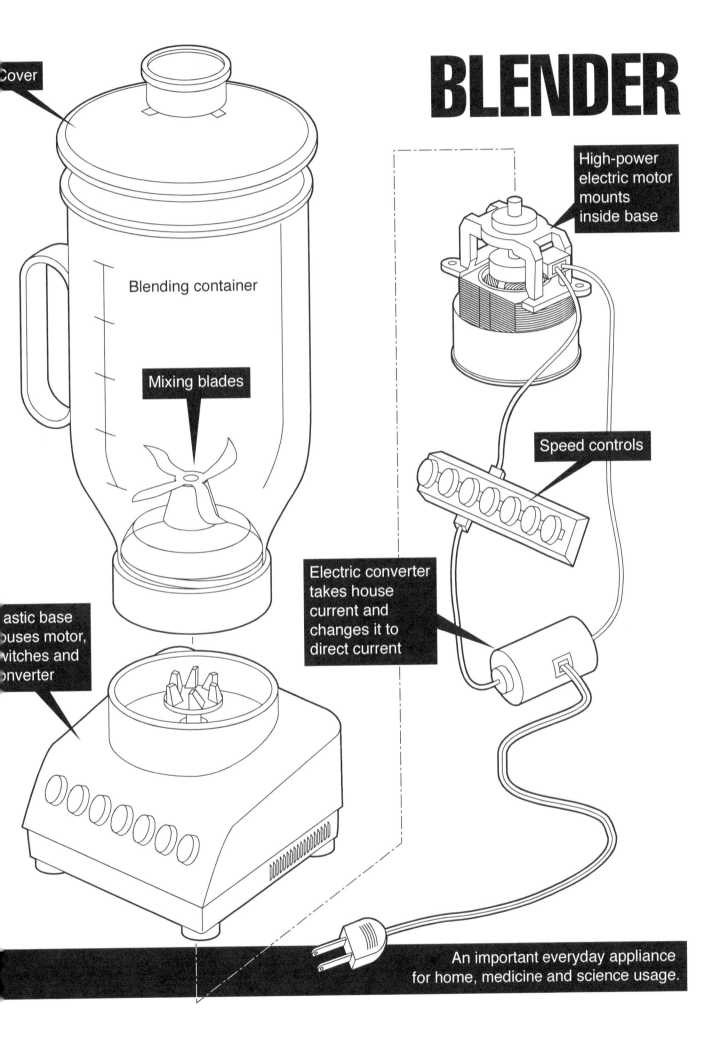

Cover

BLENDER

High-power electric motor mounts inside base

Blending container

Mixing blades

Speed controls

Electric converter takes house current and changes it to direct current

astic base
uses motor,
vitches and
onverter

An important everyday appliance
for home, medicine and science usage.

ELECTRIC GUITAR

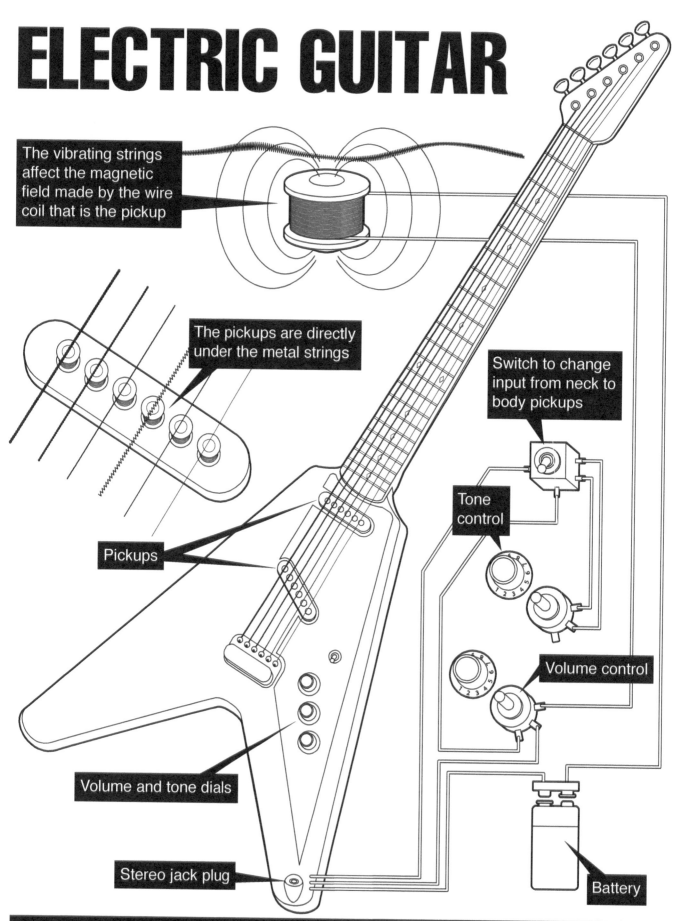

The vibrating strings affect the magnetic field made by the wire coil that is the pickup

The pickups are directly under the metal strings

Switch to change input from neck to body pickups

Tone control

Pickups

Volume control

Volume and tone dials

Stereo jack plug

Battery

Invented in 1931 - to be loud enough to be heard in a full jazz band, it was adopted by Blues musicians and then by Rock and Rollers, becoming the most important instrument in pop music.

EXTINGUISHER

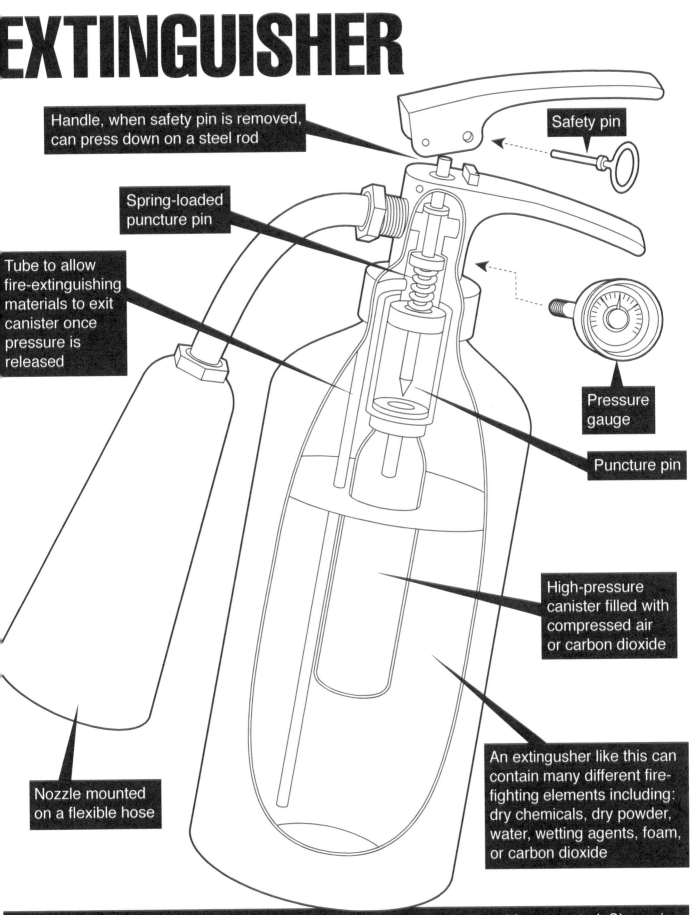

Handle, when safety pin is removed, can press down on a steel rod

Safety pin

Spring-loaded puncture pin

Tube to allow fire-extinguishing materials to exit canister once pressure is released

Pressure gauge

Puncture pin

High-pressure canister filled with compressed air or carbon dioxide

Nozzle mounted on a flexible hose

An extingusher like this can contain many different fire-fighting elements including: dry chemicals, dry powder, water, wetting agents, foam, or carbon dioxide

There are two main types of fire extinguishers: stored pressure and cartridge-operated. Shown is a small hand-held cartridge model that would weigh under 20 pounds.

BREADMAKER

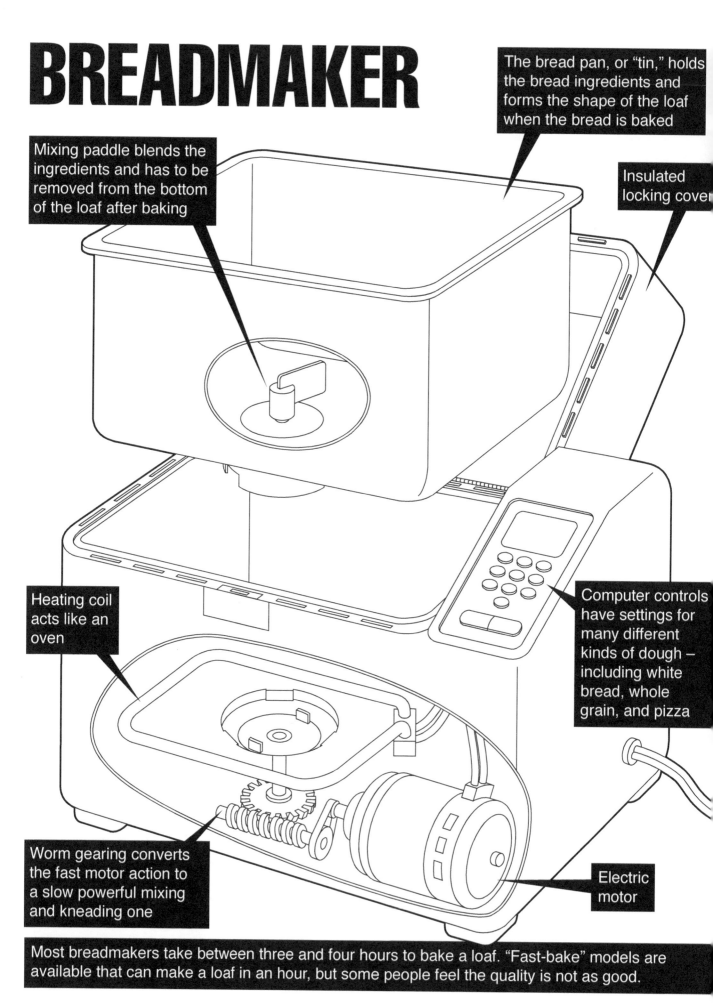

The bread pan, or "tin," holds the bread ingredients and forms the shape of the loaf when the bread is baked

Mixing paddle blends the ingredients and has to be removed from the bottom of the loaf after baking

Insulated locking cover

Heating coil acts like an oven

Computer controls have settings for many different kinds of dough – including white bread, whole grain, and pizza

Worm gearing converts the fast motor action to a slow powerful mixing and kneading one

Electric motor

Most breadmakers take between three and four hours to bake a loaf. "Fast-bake" models are available that can make a loaf in an hour, but some people feel the quality is not as good.

DIGITAL CAMERA

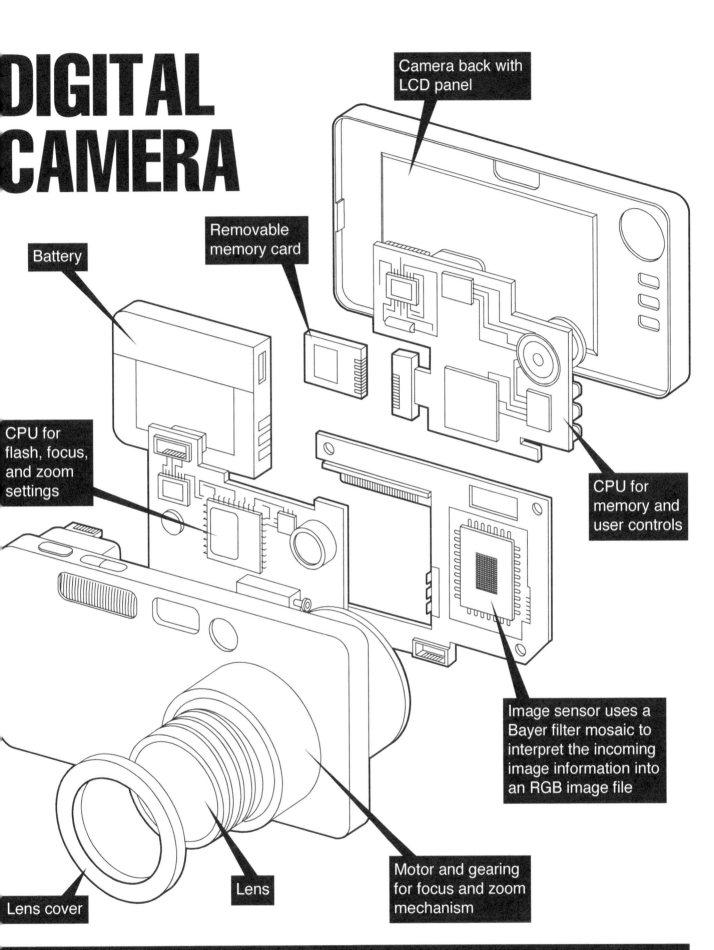

Camera back with LCD panel

Removable memory card

Battery

CPU for flash, focus, and zoom settings

CPU for memory and user controls

Image sensor uses a Bayer filter mosaic to interpret the incoming image information into an RGB image file

Lens cover

Lens

Motor and gearing for focus and zoom mechanism

A Point-and-Shoot camera is designed for easy use - to capture simple "snapshots" and take short low-resolution movies with sound.

DISHWASHER

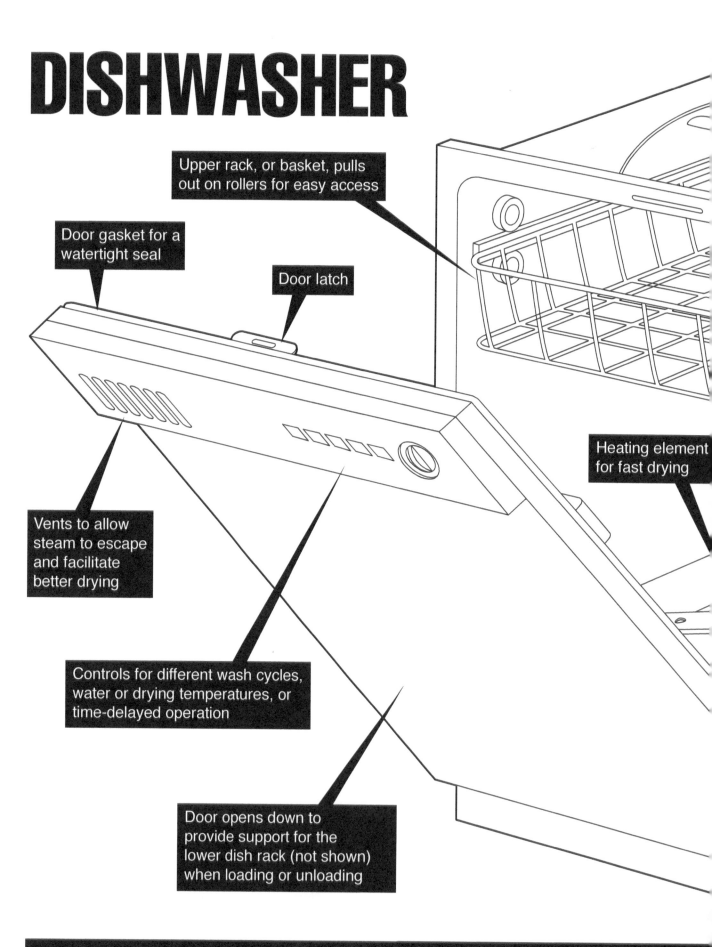

Upper rack, or basket, pulls out on rollers for easy access

Door gasket for a watertight seal

Door latch

Heating element for fast drying

Vents to allow steam to escape and facilitate better drying

Controls for different wash cycles, water or drying temperatures, or time-delayed operation

Door opens down to provide support for the lower dish rack (not shown) when loading or unloading

CLEANING BY SPRAYING

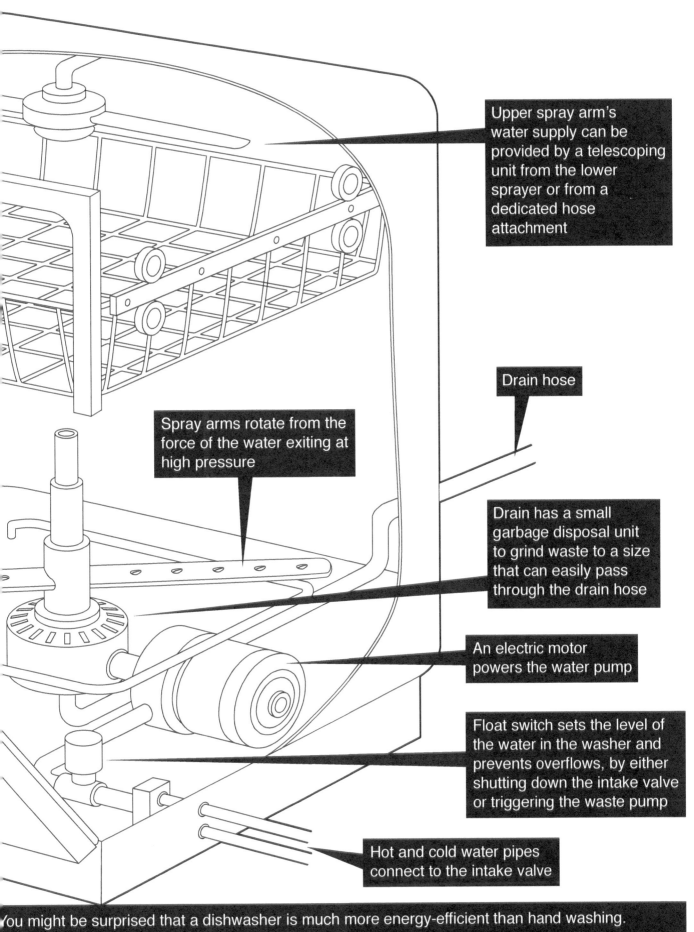

Upper spray arm's water supply can be provided by a telescoping unit from the lower sprayer or from a dedicated hose attachment

Drain hose

Spray arms rotate from the force of the water exiting at high pressure

Drain has a small garbage disposal unit to grind waste to a size that can easily pass through the drain hose

An electric motor powers the water pump

Float switch sets the level of the water in the washer and prevents overflows, by either shutting down the intake valve or triggering the waste pump

Hot and cold water pipes connect to the intake valve

You might be surprised that a dishwasher is much more energy-efficient than hand washing. With modern versions, manual pre-rinsing is also not necessary.

CEILING FAN

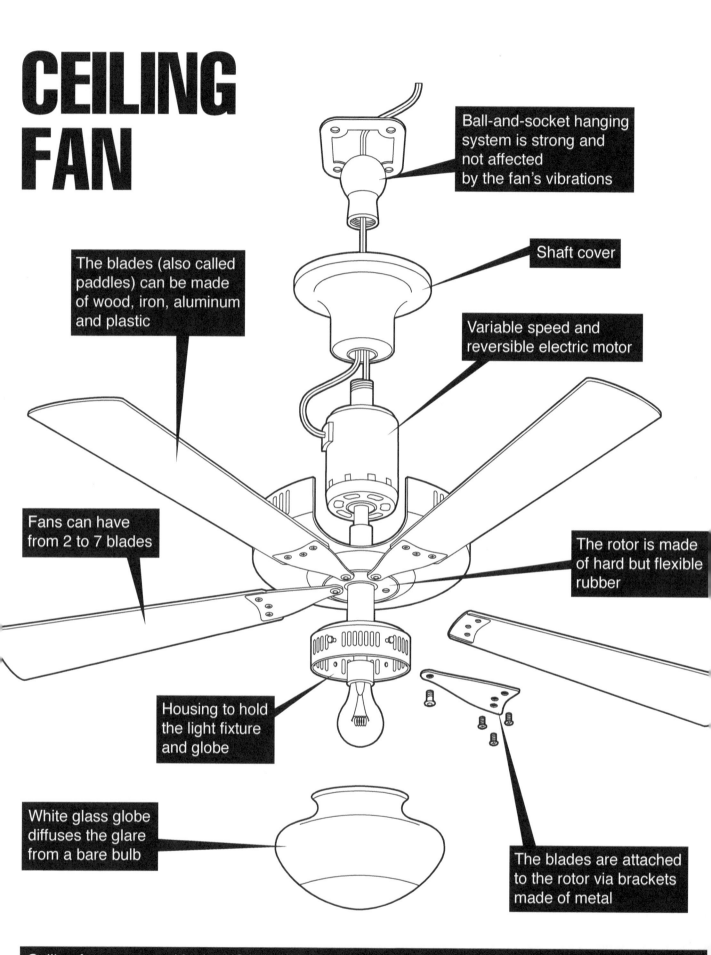

Ball-and-socket hanging system is strong and not affected by the fan's vibrations

Shaft cover

The blades (also called paddles) can be made of wood, iron, aluminum and plastic

Variable speed and reversible electric motor

Fans can have from 2 to 7 blades

The rotor is made of hard but flexible rubber

Housing to hold the light fixture and globe

White glass globe diffuses the glare from a bare bulb

The blades are attached to the rotor via brackets made of metal

Ceiling fans appeared in the USA during the early 1860s - mainly in stores, restaurants, & offices. They are very popular in homes today for their ecological cooling effect and varied design styles.

CELL PHONE

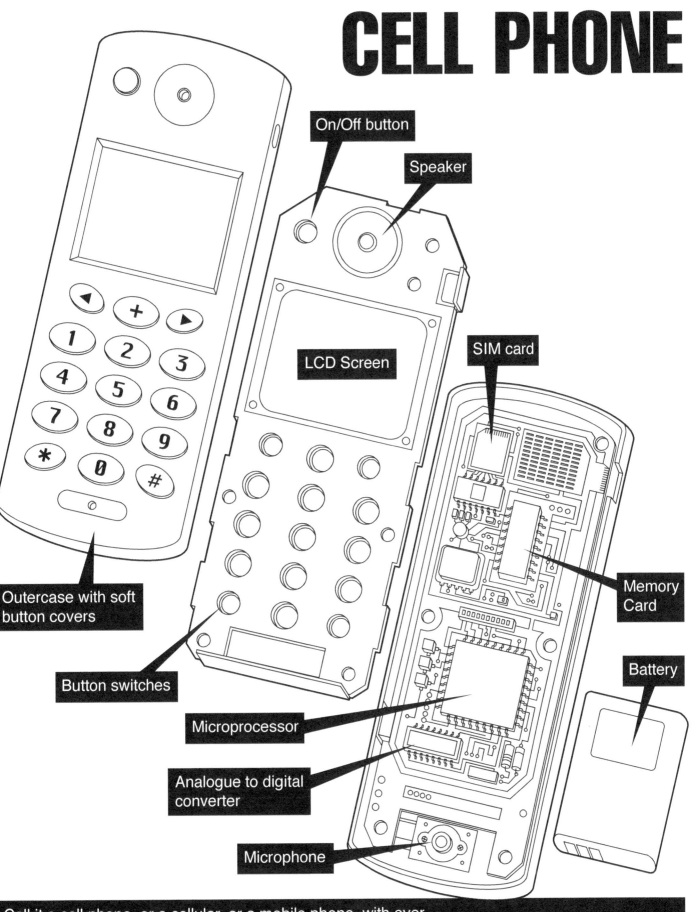

On/Off button

Speaker

LCD Screen

SIM card

Memory Card

Battery

Outercase with soft button covers

Button switches

Microprocessor

Analogue to digital converter

Microphone

Call it a cell phone, or a cellular, or a mobile phone, with over six billion users, it has taken over the world unlike any other electronic device.

CHAINSAW

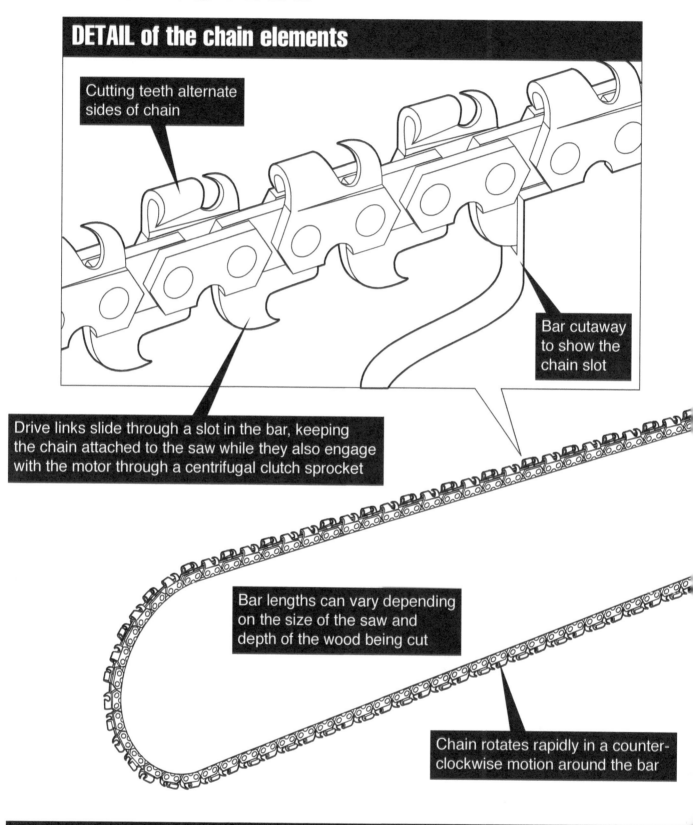

DETAIL of the chain elements

Cutting teeth alternate sides of chain

Bar cutaway to show the chain slot

Drive links slide through a slot in the bar, keeping the chain attached to the saw while they also engage with the motor through a centrifugal clutch sprocket

Bar lengths can vary depending on the size of the saw and depth of the wood being cut

Chain rotates rapidly in a counter-clockwise motion around the bar

A CUTTING-EDGE TOOL

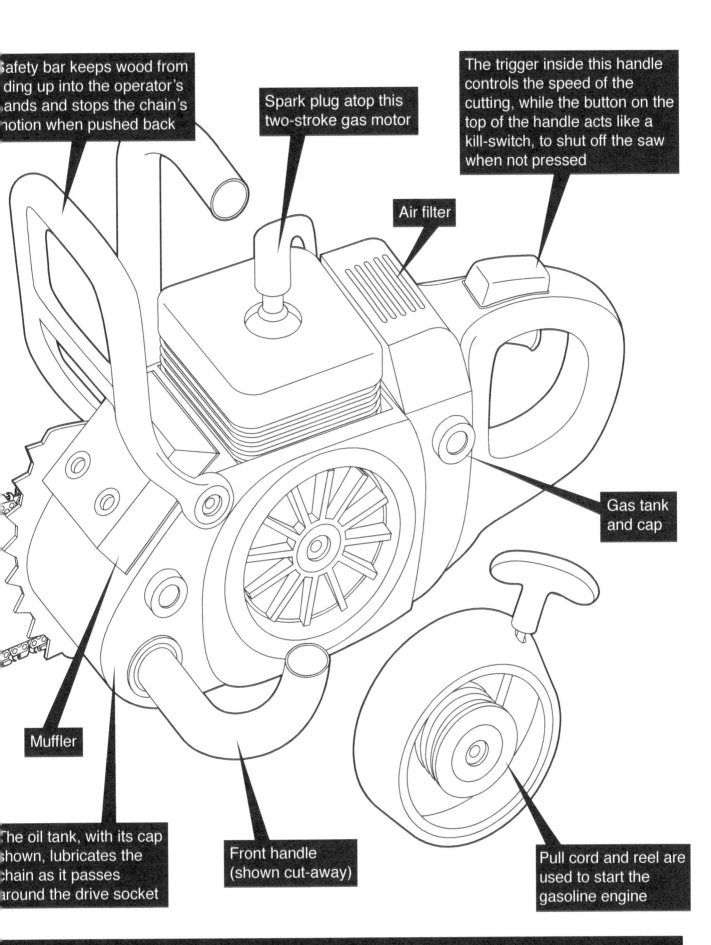

Safety bar keeps wood from [bin]ding up into the operator's [h]ands and stops the chain's [m]otion when pushed back

Spark plug atop this two-stroke gas motor

The trigger inside this handle controls the speed of the cutting, while the button on the top of the handle acts like a kill-switch, to shut off the saw when not pressed

Air filter

Gas tank and cap

Muffler

[T]he oil tank, with its cap [s]hown, lubricates the [c]hain as it passes [a]round the drive socket

Front handle (shown cut-away)

Pull cord and reel are used to start the gasoline engine

[W]hether powered by an electric motor, or a gas engine like the example shown, no tool has made [th]e cutting of trees easier. They have been adapted to cut stone, concrete, and, in Finland, ice.

CLOTHES DRYER

Lint trap captures loose particles and must be cleared to prevent fire from heat build-up

Belt powered by the motor rotates the tumble drum

Door has switch to turn off tumbler when opened

Rollers on which the drum rotates

Pulley to keep the drumbelt tensioned

FORCED AIR TUMBLER

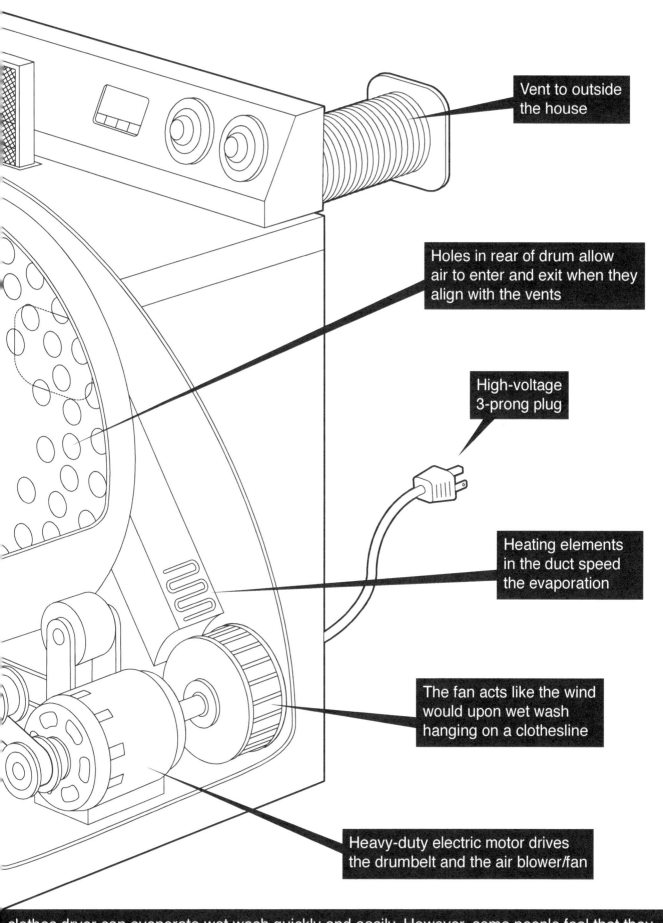

Vent to outside the house

Holes in rear of drum allow air to enter and exit when they align with the vents

High-voltage 3-prong plug

Heating elements in the duct speed the evaporation

The fan acts like the wind would upon wet wash hanging on a clothesline

Heavy-duty electric motor drives the drumbelt and the air blower/fan

clothes dryer can evaporate wet wash quickly and easily. However, some people feel that they hrink and harden clothing fibers, so they still hang their wash out on lines to dry.

FLASHLIGHT

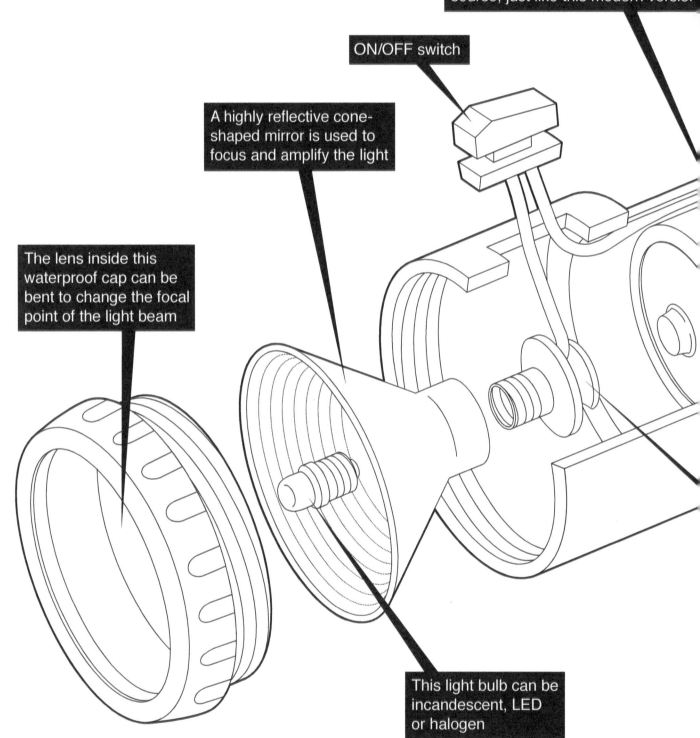

The original 1899 patent version of this style of flashlight used 2 alkaline D batteries as the power source, just like this modern version

ON/OFF switch

A highly reflective cone-shaped mirror is used to focus and amplify the light

The lens inside this waterproof cap can be bent to change the focal point of the light beam

This light bulb can be incandescent, LED or halogen

LIGHT WHEN YOU NEED IT

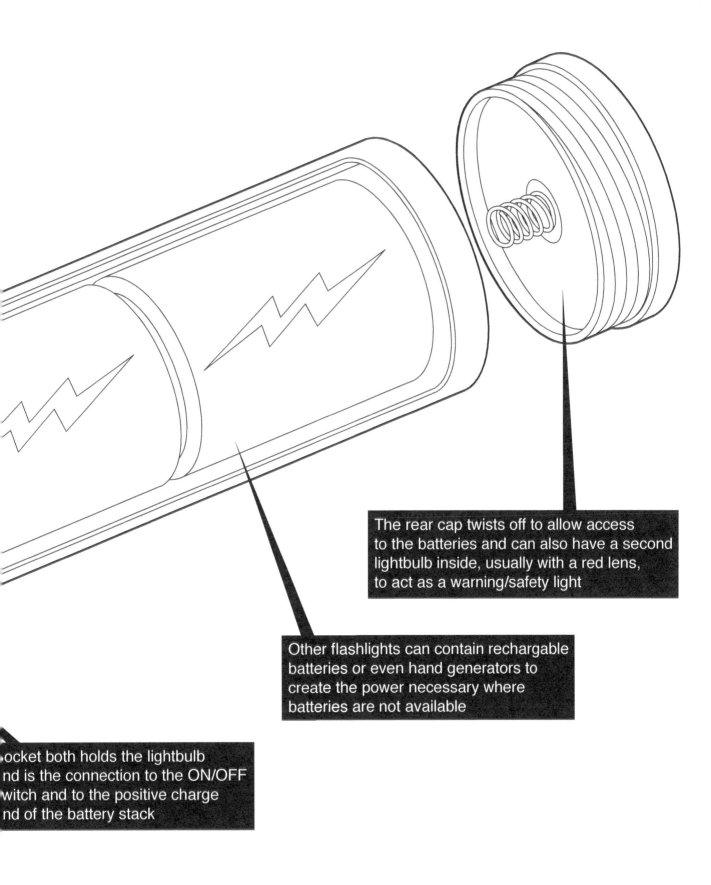

The rear cap twists off to allow access to the batteries and can also have a second lightbulb inside, usually with a red lens, to act as a warning/safety light

Other flashlights can contain rechargable batteries or even hand generators to create the power necessary where batteries are not available

ocket both holds the lightbulb
nd is the connection to the ON/OFF
witch and to the positive charge
nd of the battery stack

so called a torch, a flashlight is one of the most simple and popular electric-powered tools in the
orld. This modern example still looks like, and uses, most of the parts found in the original design.

HAIR DRYER

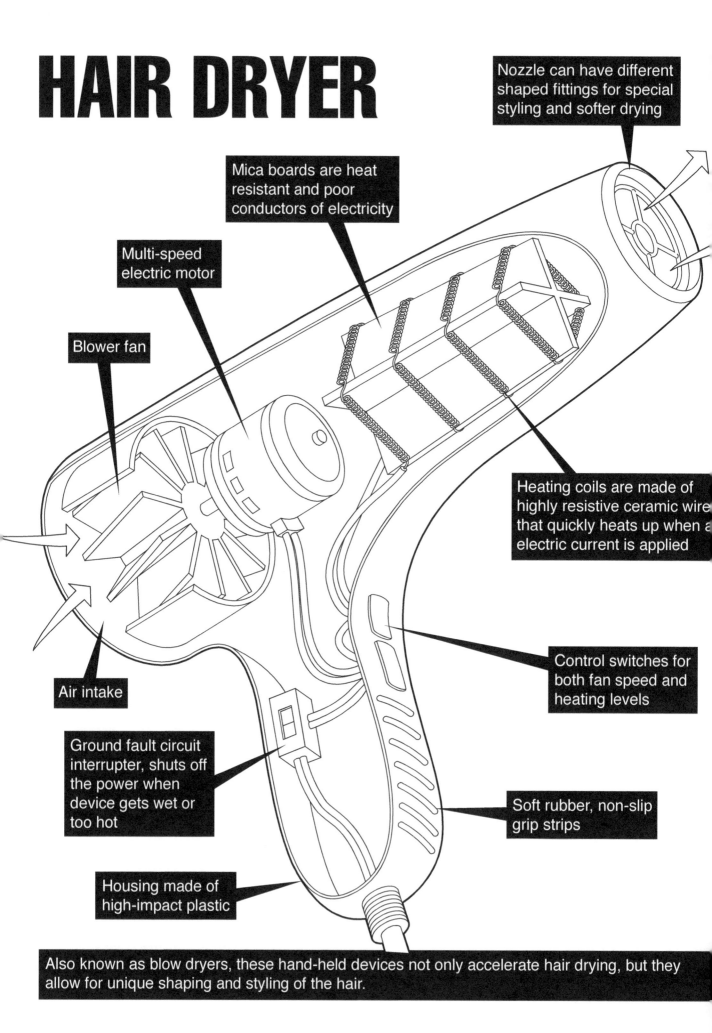

Nozzle can have different shaped fittings for special styling and softer drying

Mica boards are heat resistant and poor conductors of electricity

Multi-speed electric motor

Blower fan

Heating coils are made of highly resistive ceramic wire that quickly heats up when an electric current is applied

Air intake

Control switches for both fan speed and heating levels

Ground fault circuit interrupter, shuts off the power when device gets wet or too hot

Soft rubber, non-slip grip strips

Housing made of high-impact plastic

Also known as blow dryers, these hand-held devices not only accelerate hair drying, but they allow for unique shaping and styling of the hair.

ELECTRIC HAND MIXER

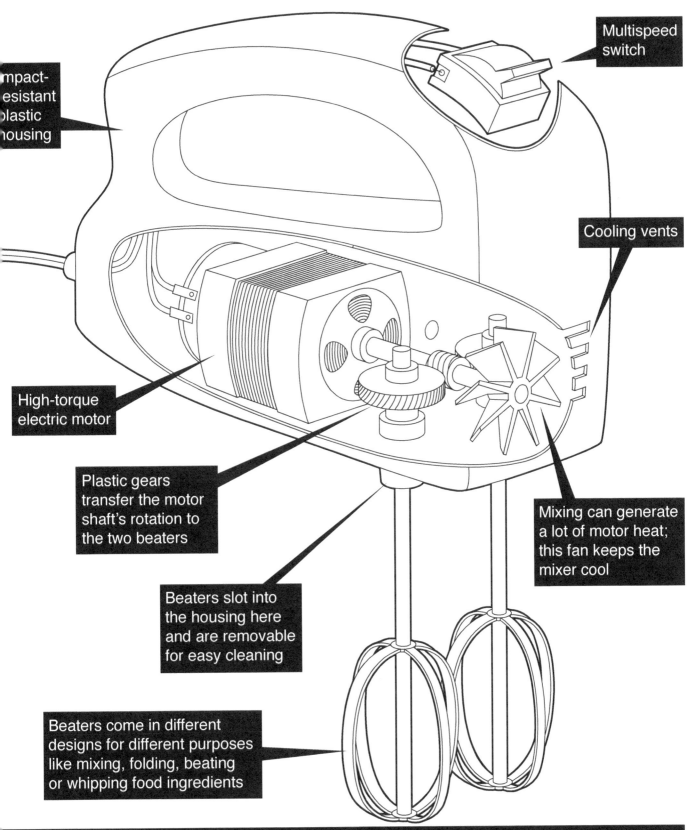

Multispeed switch

Impact-resistant plastic housing

Cooling vents

High-torque electric motor

Plastic gears transfer the motor shaft's rotation to the two beaters

Mixing can generate a lot of motor heat; this fan keeps the mixer cool

Beaters slot into the housing here and are removable for easy cleaning

Beaters come in different designs for different purposes like mixing, folding, beating or whipping food ingredients

Adapted from hand-cranked mixers, the electric hand mixer is one of the most common small appliances found in modern kitchens everywhere.

HEARING AID

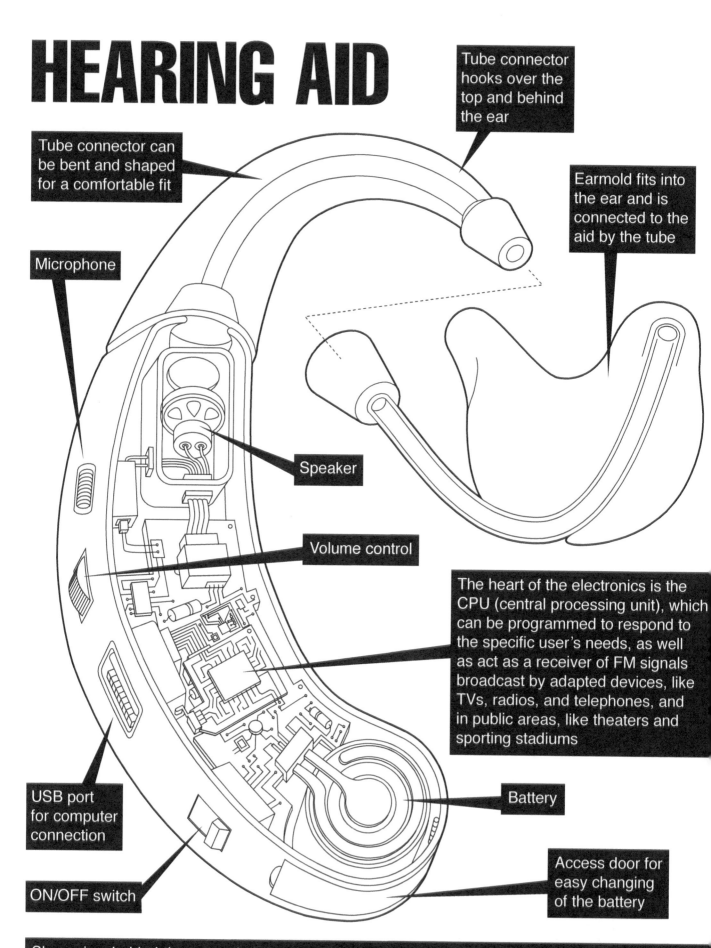

Tube connector hooks over the top and behind the ear

Tube connector can be bent and shaped for a comfortable fit

Earmold fits into the ear and is connected to the aid by the tube

Microphone

Speaker

Volume control

The heart of the electronics is the CPU (central processing unit), which can be programmed to respond to the specific user's needs, as well as act as a receiver of FM signals broadcast by adapted devices, like TVs, radios, and telephones, and in public areas, like theaters and sporting stadiums

USB port for computer connection

Battery

ON/OFF switch

Access door for easy changing of the battery

Shown is a behind-the-ear-style hearing aid for people with mild to extreme hearing loss. This is the most durabile style of aid as the electronics are kept away from ear moisture and earwax.

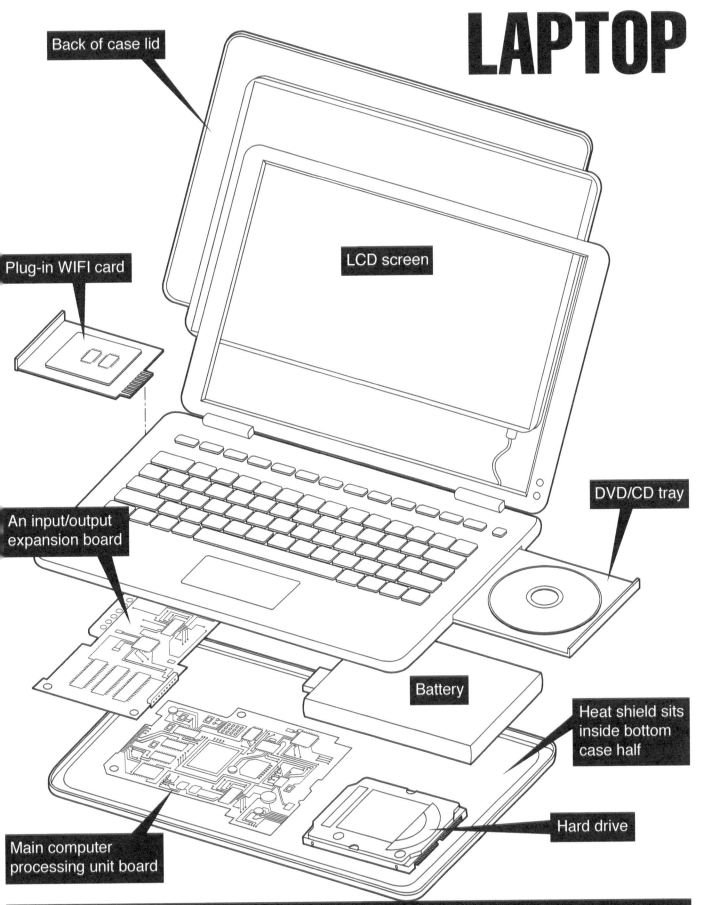

LAPTOP

Back of case lid

LCD screen

Plug-in WIFI card

An input/output expansion board

DVD/CD tray

Battery

Heat shield sits inside bottom case half

Hard drive

Main computer processing unit board

A portable computer with all the features of a desktop system, the laptop allows a person to take games or classroom or office work everywhere.

GARBAGE DISPOSAL

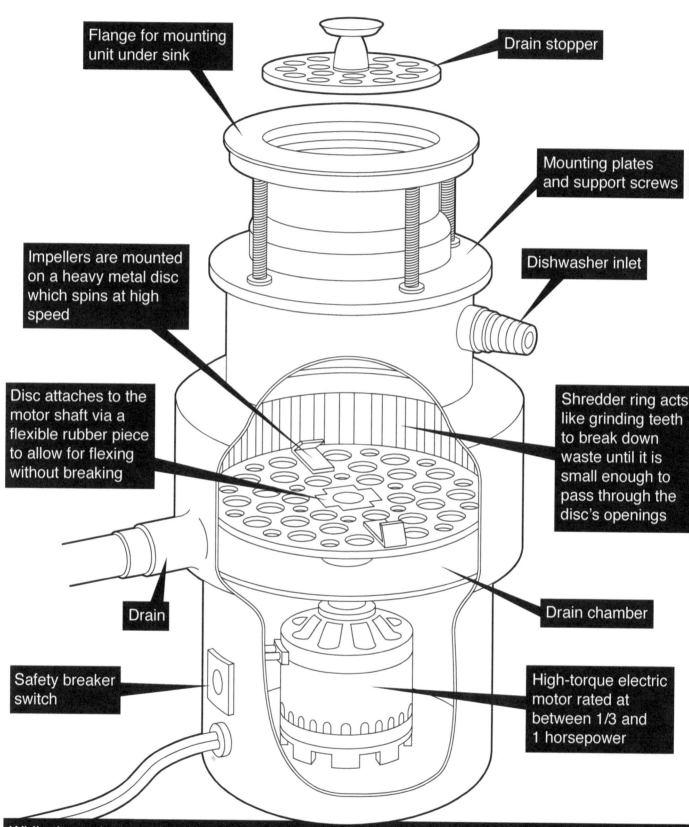

Flange for mounting unit under sink

Drain stopper

Mounting plates and support screws

Impellers are mounted on a heavy metal disc which spins at high speed

Dishwasher inlet

Disc attaches to the motor shaft via a flexible rubber piece to allow for flexing without breaking

Shredder ring acts like grinding teeth to break down waste until it is small enough to pass through the disc's openings

Drain

Drain chamber

Safety breaker switch

High-torque electric motor rated at between 1/3 and 1 horsepower

While these devices are popular in the United States, they are fairly rare elsewhere. There also continues to be discussion as to whether these machines are ecologically good or bad.

AIR CONDITIONER

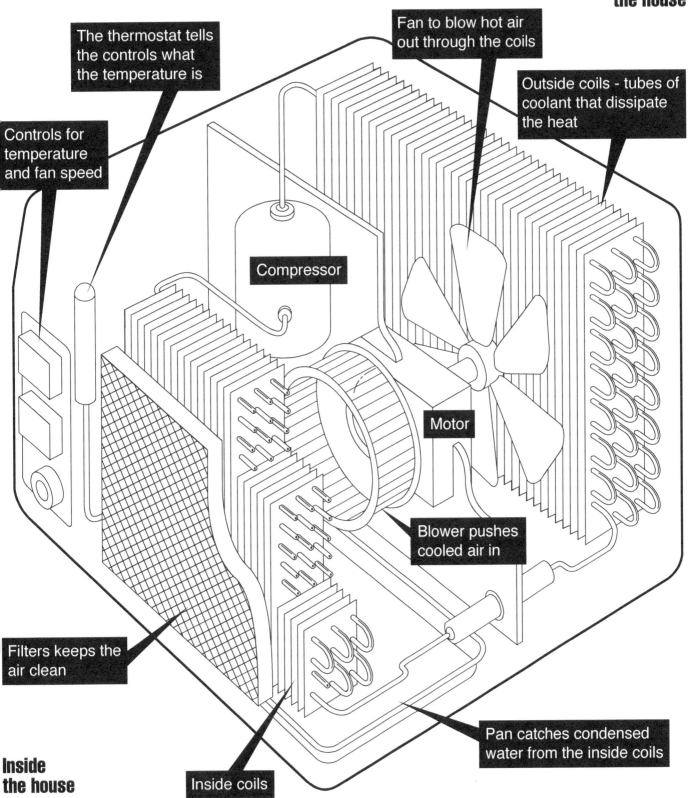

The thermostat tells the controls what the temperature is

Fan to blow hot air out through the coils

Outside coils - tubes of coolant that dissipate the heat

Controls for temperature and fan speed

Compressor

Motor

Blower pushes cooled air in

Filters keeps the air clean

Pan catches condensed water from the inside coils

Inside the house

Inside coils

The introduction of an effective air conditioner, like this window unit, signaled the start of a way for everybody to keep cool in the summer.

LEAF BLOWER

Plastic housing with shaped hand grip areas for easy control of the machine during operation

Some designs have a shaped nozzle to help direct the airflow for better control

Air speed inside nozzle tube can reach 140 miles per hour

Nozzle length can run between 2.5 and 4 ft. long

Nozzle is detachable from blower

AIR-POWERED GARDENING

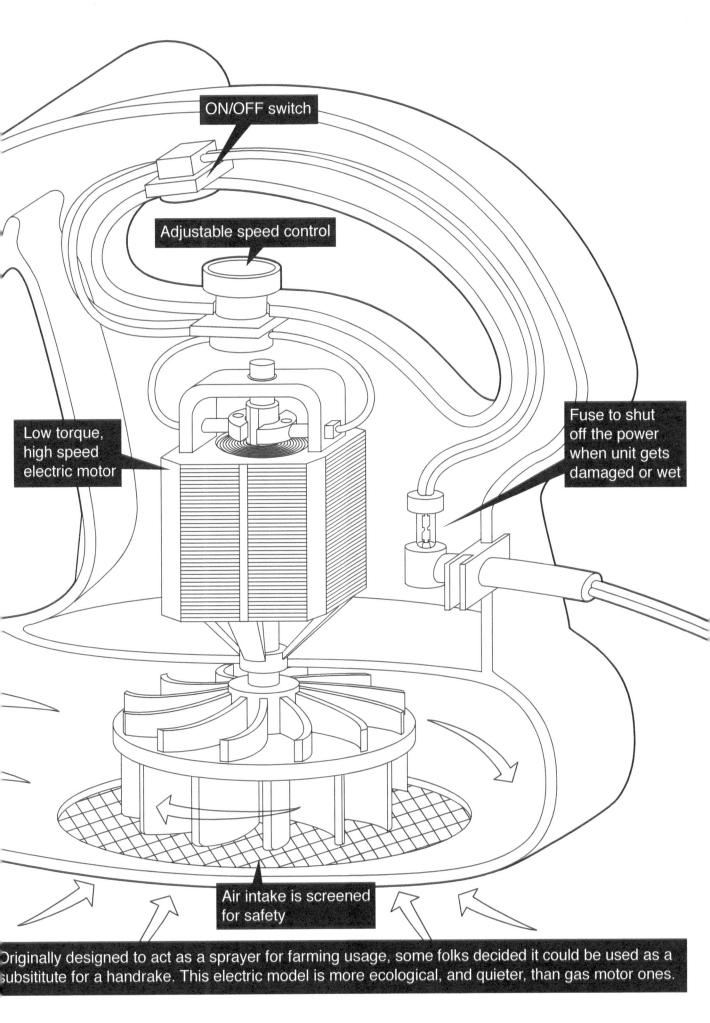

ON/OFF switch

Adjustable speed control

Low torque,
high speed
electric motor

Fuse to shut
off the power
when unit gets
damaged or wet

Air intake is screened
for safety

Originally designed to act as a sprayer for farming usage, some folks decided it could be used as a subsititute for a handrake. This electric model is more ecological, and quieter, than gas motor ones.

MICROWAVE OVEN

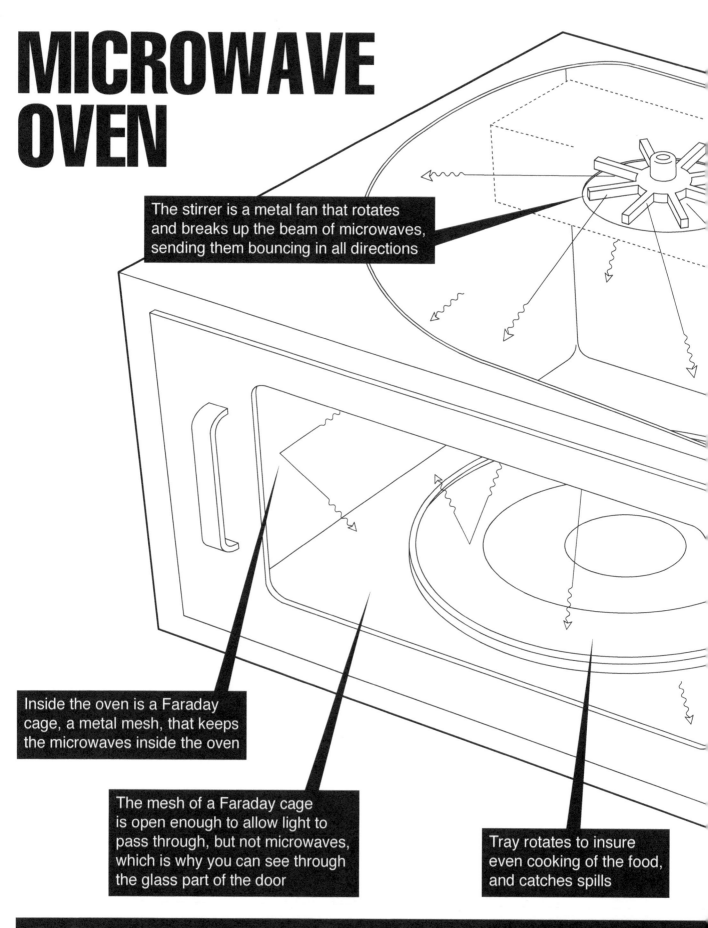

The stirrer is a metal fan that rotates and breaks up the beam of microwaves, sending them bouncing in all directions

Inside the oven is a Faraday cage, a metal mesh, that keeps the microwaves inside the oven

The mesh of a Faraday cage is open enough to allow light to pass through, but not microwaves, which is why you can see through the glass part of the door

Tray rotates to insure even cooking of the food, and catches spills

DIELECTRIC COOKING

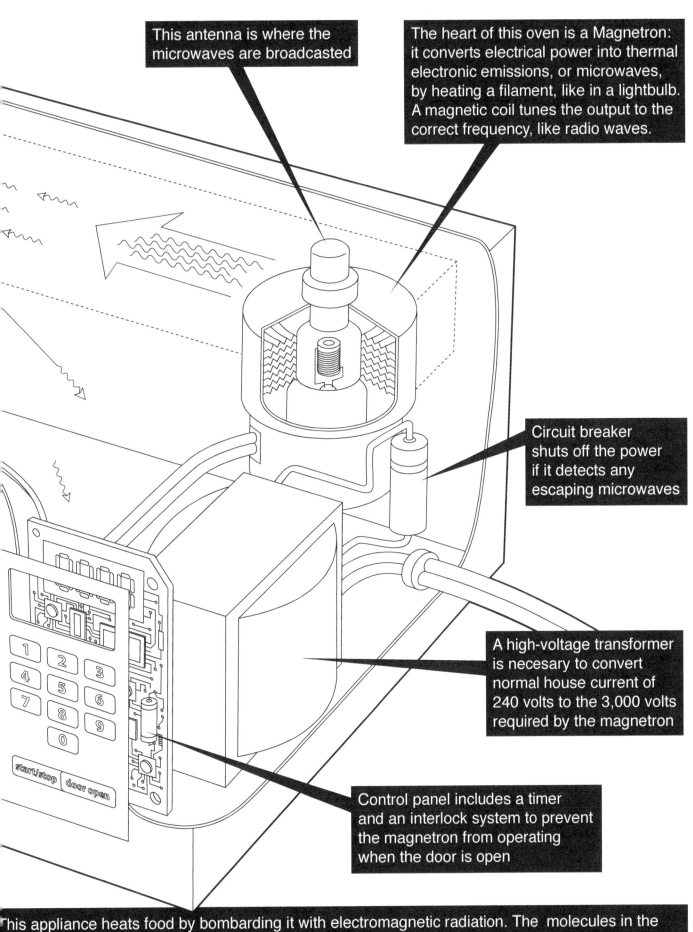

This antenna is where the microwaves are broadcasted

The heart of this oven is a Magnetron: it converts electrical power into thermal electronic emissions, or microwaves, by heating a filament, like in a lightbulb. A magnetic coil tunes the output to the correct frequency, like radio waves.

Circuit breaker shuts off the power if it detects any escaping microwaves

A high-voltage transformer is necesary to convert normal house current of 240 volts to the 3,000 volts required by the magnetron

Control panel includes a timer and an interlock system to prevent the magnetron from operating when the door is open

This appliance heats food by bombarding it with electromagnetic radiation. The molecules in the food become excited, or hot, in a process known as dielectric heating.

HOT TUB

Nozzles for water jets can be adjusted for different forces and tempratures

Air blower forces air into water vents to create bubble effect

Natural gas or electric heater

Filtration unit removes particles from the water and ionizes them to help kill bacteria

Water Pump

A RELAXING SOAK

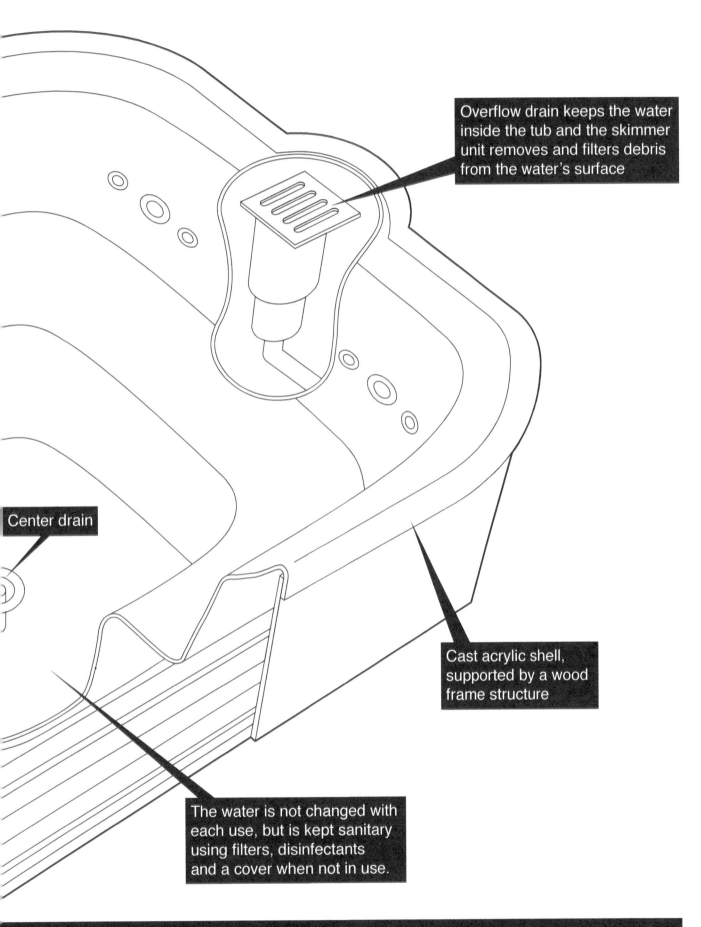

Overflow drain keeps the water inside the tub and the skimmer unit removes and filters debris from the water's surface

Center drain

Cast acrylic shell, supported by a wood frame structure

The water is not changed with each use, but is kept sanitary using filters, disinfectants and a cover when not in use.

Unlike a typical bathtub, a hot tub is designed to be used by more than one person at a time and is usually located outdoors.

SEWING MACHINE

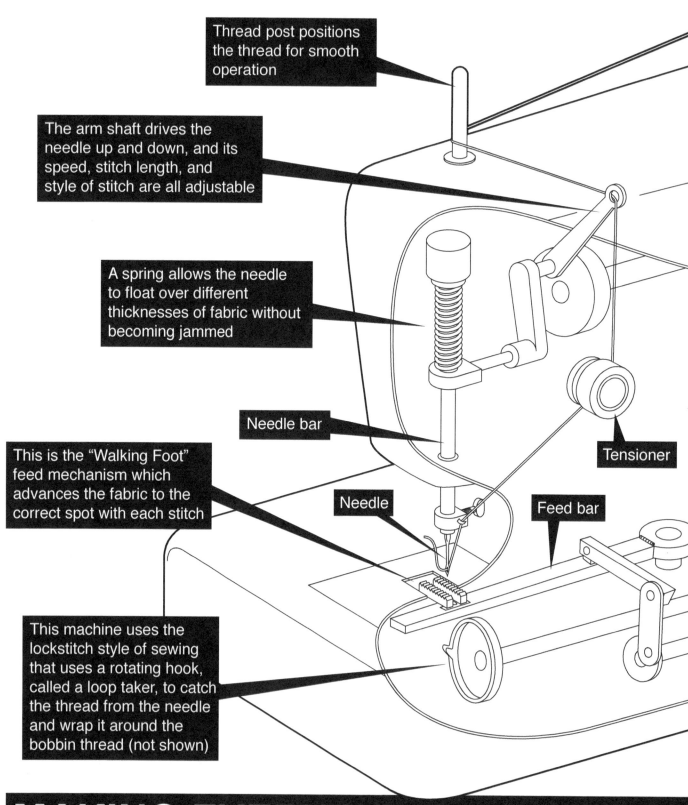

Thread post positions the thread for smooth operation

The arm shaft drives the needle up and down, and its speed, stitch length, and style of stitch are all adjustable

A spring allows the needle to float over different thicknesses of fabric without becoming jammed

Needle bar

Tensioner

This is the "Walking Foot" feed mechanism which advances the fabric to the correct spot with each stitch

Needle

Feed bar

This machine uses the lockstitch style of sewing that uses a rotating hook, called a loop taker, to catch the thread from the needle and wrap it around the bobbin thread (not shown)

MAKING EVERYTHING YOU WEAR

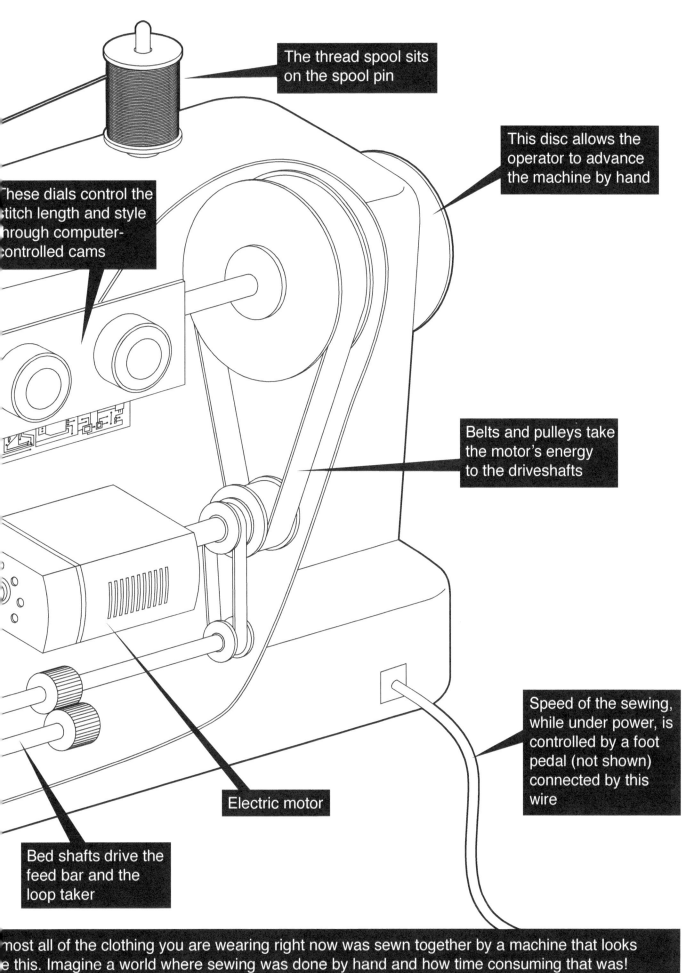

The thread spool sits on the spool pin

This disc allows the operator to advance the machine by hand

These dials control the stitch length and style through computer-controlled cams

Belts and pulleys take the motor's energy to the driveshafts

Speed of the sewing, while under power, is controlled by a foot pedal (not shown) connected by this wire

Electric motor

Bed shafts drive the feed bar and the loop taker

most all of the clothing you are wearing right now was sewn together by a machine that looks e this. Imagine a world where sewing was done by hand and how time consuming that was!

The screen is made of many layers

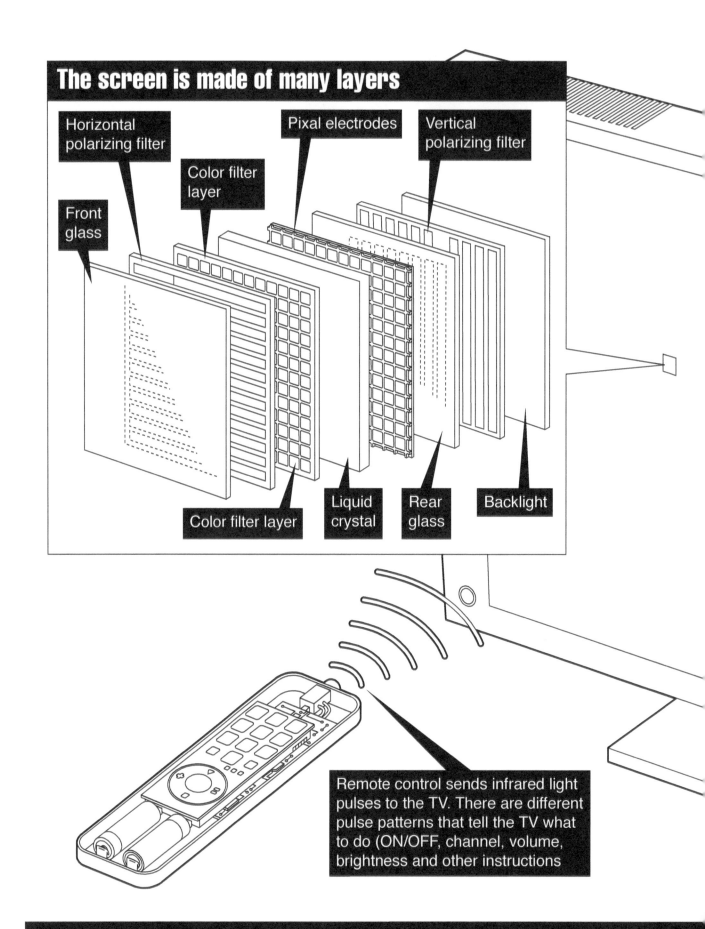

Horizontal polarizing filter

Pixal electrodes

Vertical polarizing filter

Color filter layer

Front glass

Color filter layer

Liquid crystal

Rear glass

Backlight

Remote control sends infrared light pulses to the TV. There are different pulse patterns that tell the TV what to do (ON/OFF, channel, volume, brightness and other instructions

LIQUID CRYSTAL TECHNOLOGY

FLAT PANEL TV

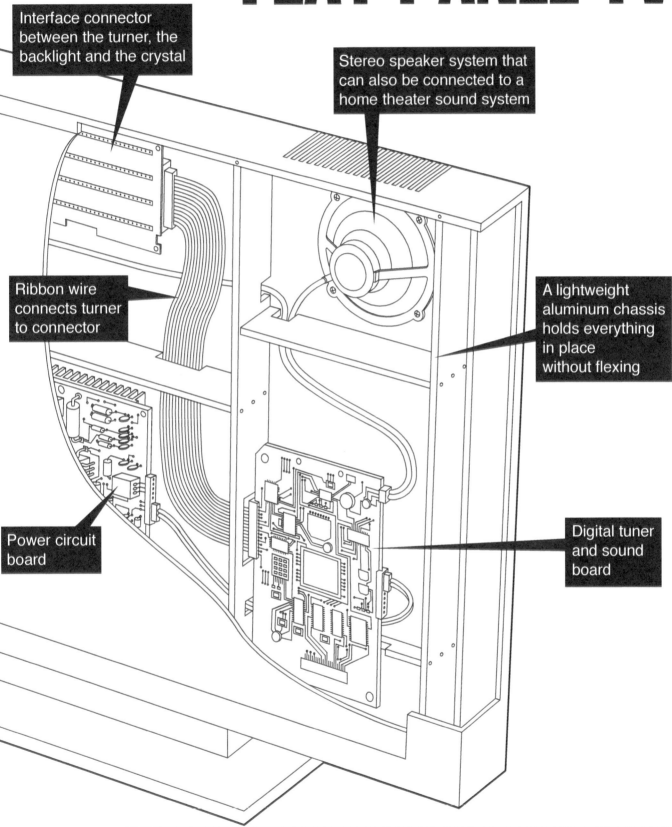

Interface connector between the turner, the backlight and the crystal

Stereo speaker system that can also be connected to a home theater sound system

Ribbon wire connects turner to connector

A lightweight aluminum chassis holds everything in place without flexing

Power circuit board

Digital tuner and sound board

ghtweight, inexpensive and easy on the eyes, an LCD display uses electricity to activate a ecial liquid crystal which changes the light polarizing properties and color filter elements.

VACUUM CLEANER

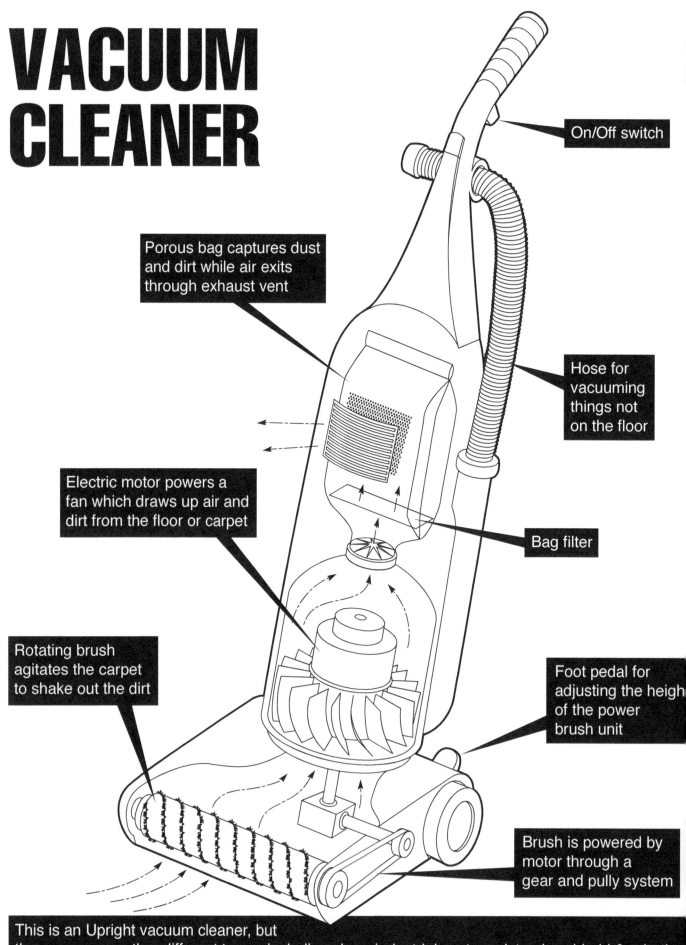

On/Off switch

Porous bag captures dust and dirt while air exits through exhaust vent

Hose for vacuuming things not on the floor

Electric motor powers a fan which draws up air and dirt from the floor or carpet

Bag filter

Rotating brush agitates the carpet to shake out the dirt

Foot pedal for adjusting the heigh of the power brush unit

Brush is powered by motor through a gear and pully system

This is an Upright vacuum cleaner, but there are many other different types, including shop, industrial, wet, canister, hand-held & robotic.

WASHING MACHINE

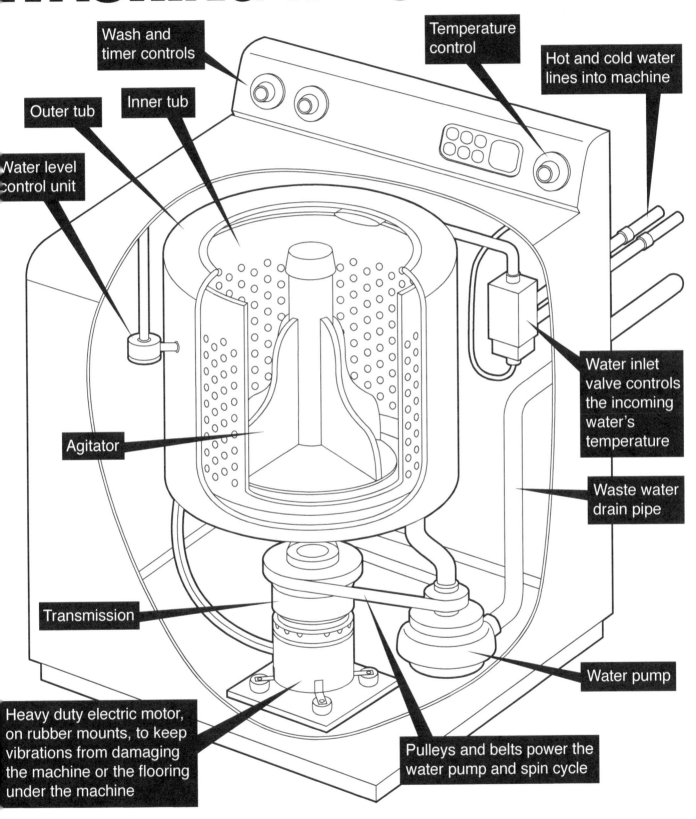

Wash and timer controls

Temperature control

Hot and cold water lines into machine

Outer tub

Inner tub

Water level control unit

Water inlet valve controls the incoming water's temperature

Agitator

Waste water drain pipe

Transmission

Water pump

Heavy duty electric motor, on rubber mounts, to keep vibrations from damaging the machine or the flooring under the machine

Pulleys and belts power the water pump and spin cycle

Before these machines arrived, one could expect to spend a whole day cleaning a week's worth of laundry. Because of this, the washer is thought of as the greatest invention of the industrial revolution.

SMOKE DETECTOR

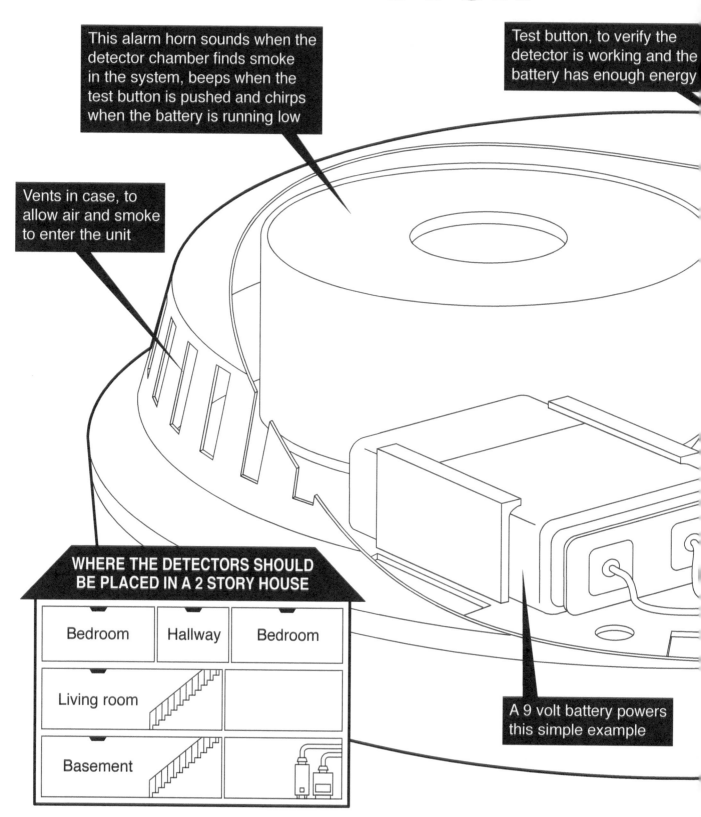

This alarm horn sounds when the detector chamber finds smoke in the system, beeps when the test button is pushed and chirps when the battery is running low

Test button, to verify the detector is working and the battery has enough energy

Vents in case, to allow air and smoke to enter the unit

WHERE THE DETECTORS SHOULD BE PLACED IN A 2 STORY HOUSE

Bedroom	Hallway	Bedroom
Living room		
Basement		

A 9 volt battery powers this simple example

PROTECTING YOUR HOME

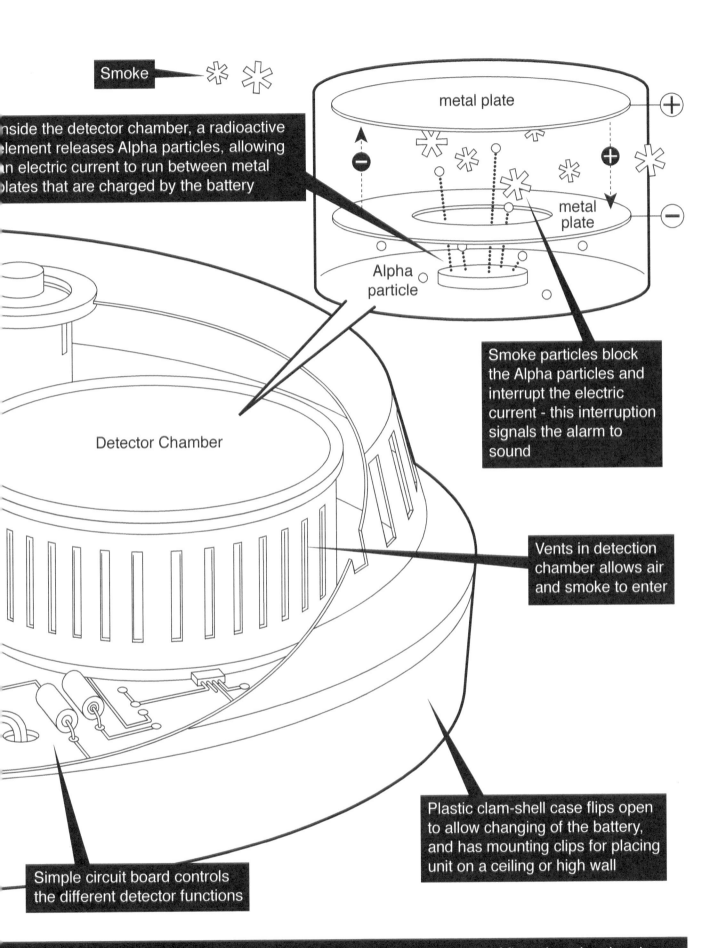

Smoke

Inside the detector chamber, a radioactive element releases Alpha particles, allowing an electric current to run between metal plates that are charged by the battery

metal plate

metal plate

Alpha particle

Smoke particles block the Alpha particles and interrupt the electric current - this interruption signals the alarm to sound

Detector Chamber

Vents in detection chamber allows air and smoke to enter

Plastic clam-shell case flips open to allow changing of the battery, and has mounting clips for placing unit on a ceiling or high wall

Simple circuit board controls the different detector functions

This device uses an ionization chamber to detect smoke as an indicator of fire, triggering the alarm to signal the danger. You should check your alarms every 6 months and replace their batteries.

SNOW BLOWER

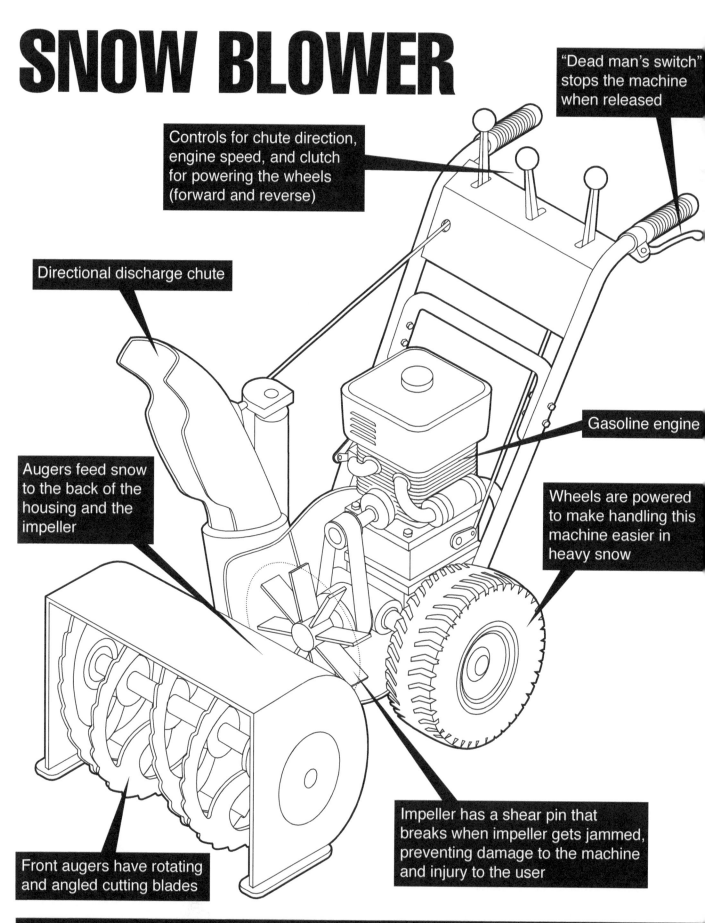

"Dead man's switch" stops the machine when released

Controls for chute direction, engine speed, and clutch for powering the wheels (forward and reverse)

Directional discharge chute

Gasoline engine

Augers feed snow to the back of the housing and the impeller

Wheels are powered to make handling this machine easier in heavy snow

Impeller has a shear pin that breaks when impeller gets jammed, preventing damage to the machine and injury to the user

Front augers have rotating and angled cutting blades

Also called a snow thrower, this is a "two-stage" machine where the front augers cut and bring the snow to the high-speed impeller, which then throws the snow away from the machine.

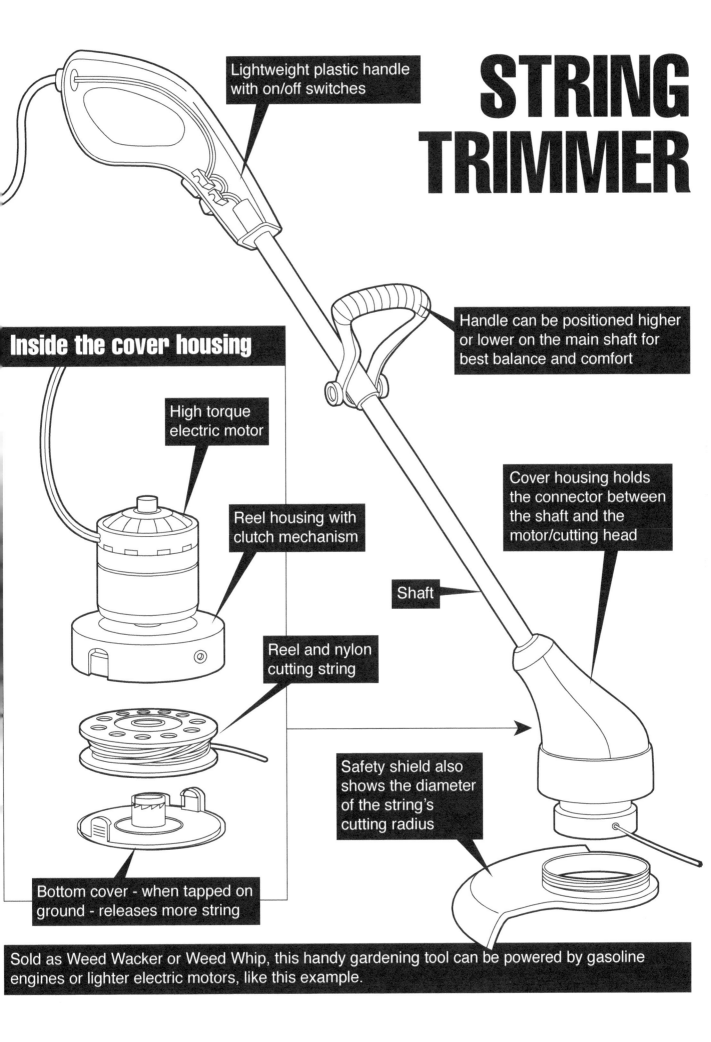

Lightweight plastic handle with on/off switches

STRING TRIMMER

Handle can be positioned higher or lower on the main shaft for best balance and comfort

Inside the cover housing

High torque electric motor

Reel housing with clutch mechanism

Cover housing holds the connector between the shaft and the motor/cutting head

Shaft

Reel and nylon cutting string

Safety shield also shows the diameter of the string's cutting radius

Bottom cover - when tapped on ground - releases more string

Sold as Weed Wacker or Weed Whip, this handy gardening tool can be powered by gasoline engines or lighter electric motors, like this example.

TABLET COMPUTER

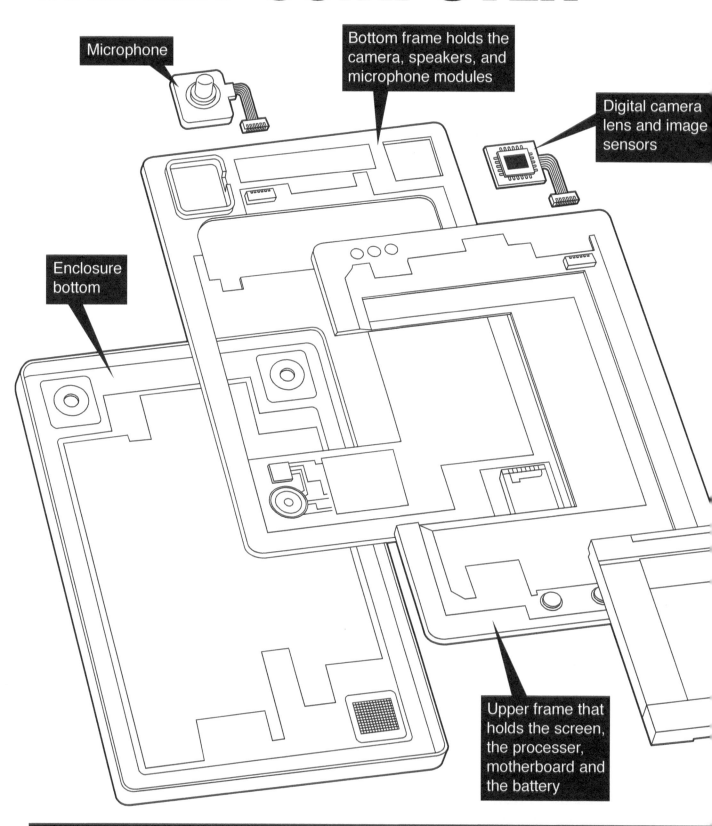

Microphone

Bottom frame holds the camera, speakers, and microphone modules

Digital camera lens and image sensors

Enclosure bottom

Upper frame that holds the screen, the processer, motherboard and the battery

TOUCHSCREEN FUN

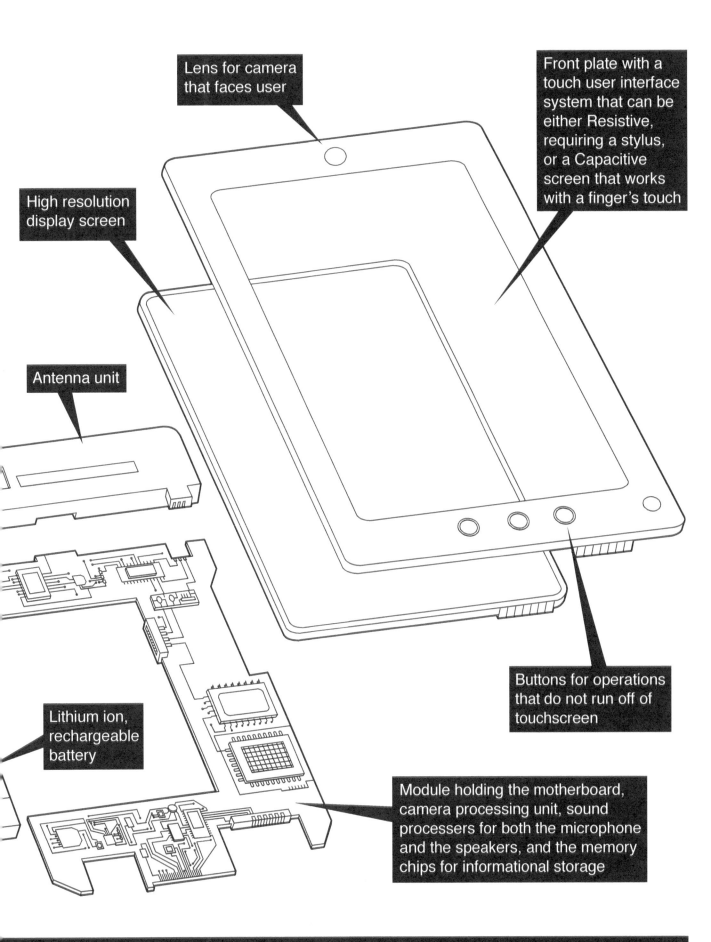

Lens for camera that faces user

Front plate with a touch user interface system that can be either Resistive, requiring a stylus, or a Capacitive screen that works with a finger's touch

High resolution display screen

Antenna unit

Buttons for operations that do not run off of touchscreen

Lithium ion, rechargeable battery

Module holding the motherboard, camera processing unit, sound processers for both the microphone and the speakers, and the memory chips for informational storage

Unlike regular computers or laptops that have keyboards, a tablet is controlled via a touchscreen, and uses a wireless connection to download web applications or games.

ELECTRIC TOOTHBRUSH

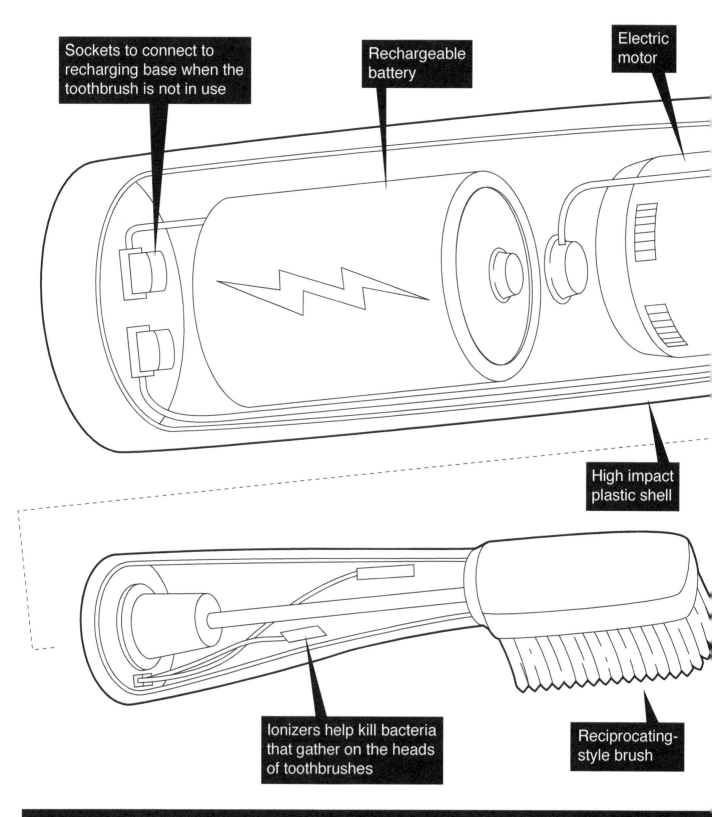

Sockets to connect to recharging base when the toothbrush is not in use

Rechargeable battery

Electric motor

High impact plastic shell

Ionizers help kill bacteria that gather on the heads of toothbrushes

Reciprocating-style brush

A CLEAN MACHINE

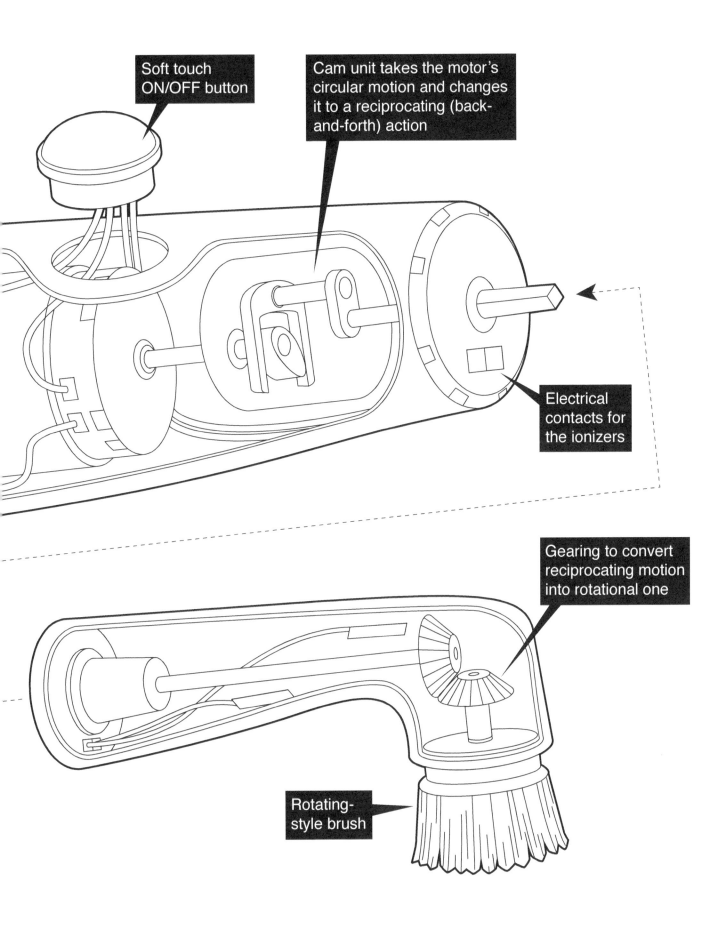

Soft touch ON/OFF button

Cam unit takes the motor's circular motion and changes it to a reciprocating (back-and-forth) action

Electrical contacts for the ionizers

Gearing to convert reciprocating motion into rotational one

Rotating-style brush

Electric brushes are classified into two styles, based on the action they employ: vibration or rotation-oscillation. We show both types here with their detachable head pieces.

SMARTPHONE

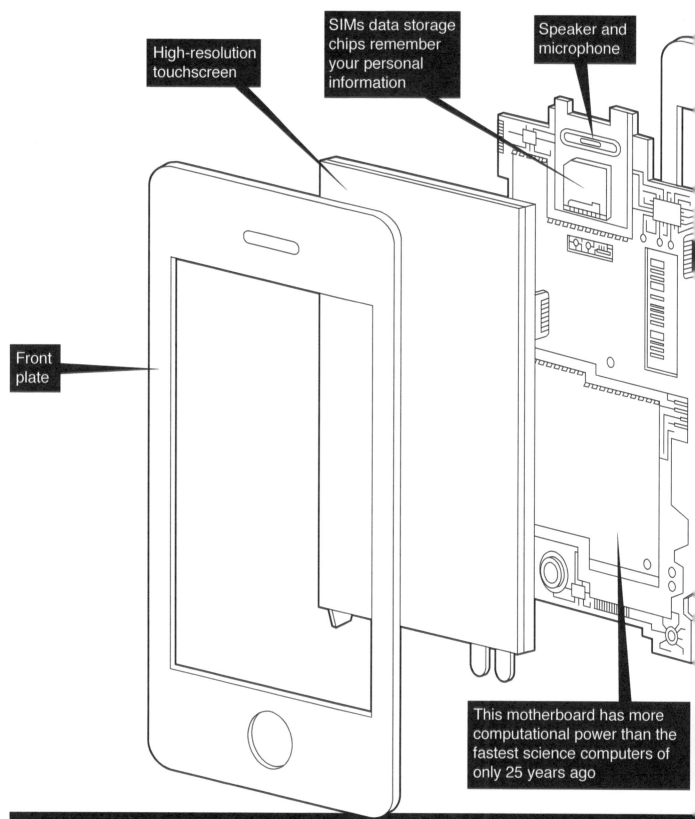

Metal frame to hold everything together

SIMs data storage chips remember your personal information

Speaker and microphone

High-resolution touchscreen

Front plate

This motherboard has more computational power than the fastest science computers of only 25 years ago

STAYING CONNECTED

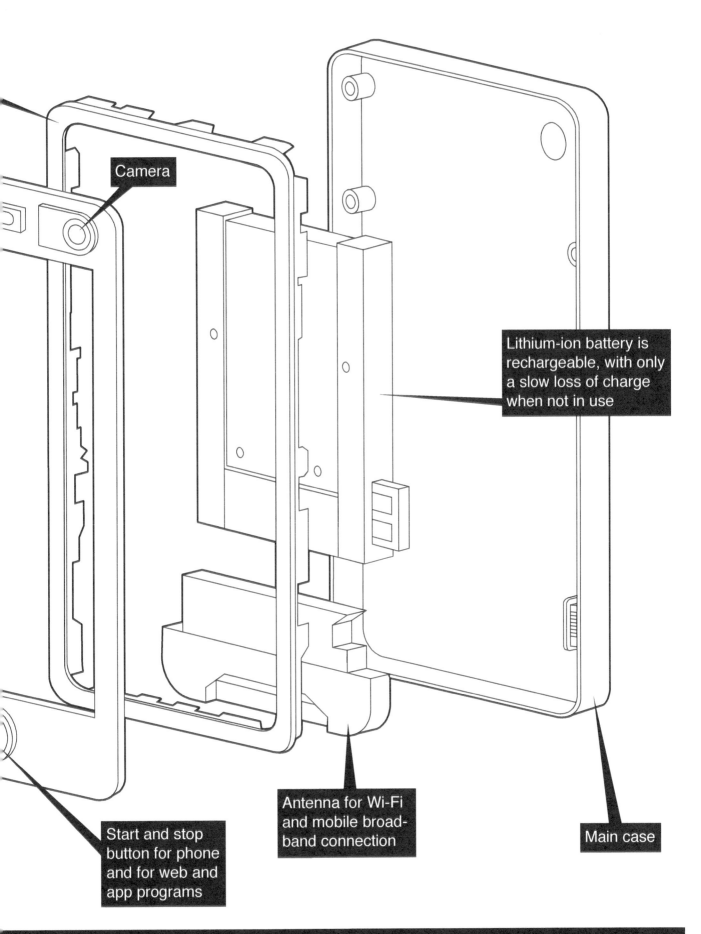

Camera

Lithium-ion battery is rechargeable, with only a slow loss of charge when not in use

Start and stop button for phone and for web and app programs

Antenna for Wi-Fi and mobile broad-band connection

Main case

A smartphone combines the functions of a personal digital assistant, media player, digital camera, video camera, mobile bank, web browser, app player, and GPS navigator into one unit.

WATER HEATER

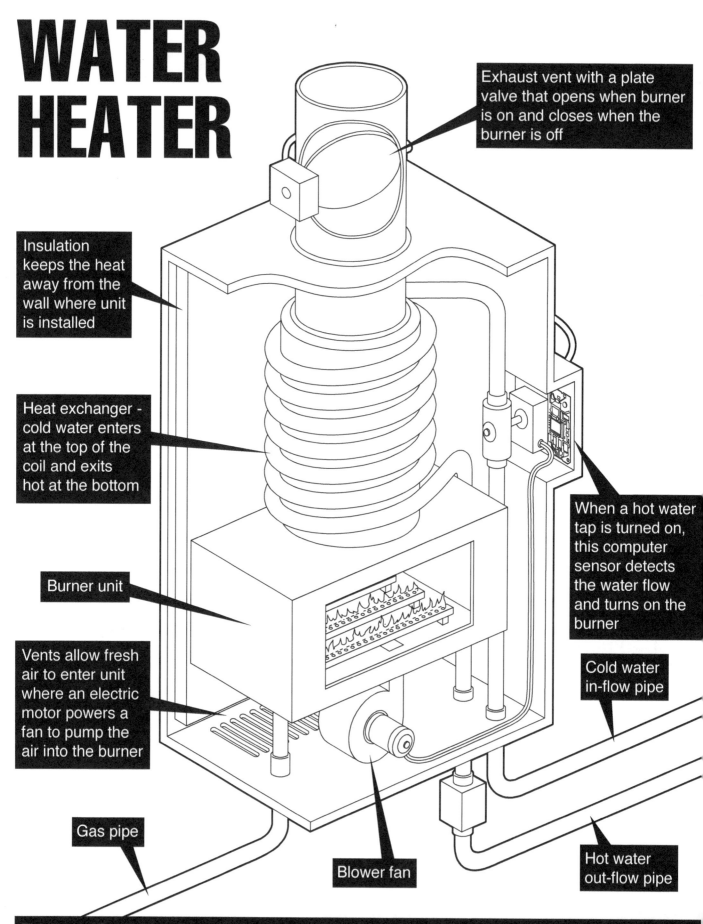

Exhaust vent with a plate valve that opens when burner is on and closes when the burner is off

Insulation keeps the heat away from the wall where unit is installed

Heat exchanger - cold water enters at the top of the coil and exits hot at the bottom

Burner unit

Vents allow fresh air to enter unit where an electric motor powers a fan to pump the air into the burner

When a hot water tap is turned on, this computer sensor detects the water flow and turns on the burner

Cold water in-flow pipe

Gas pipe

Blower fan

Hot water out-flow pipe

This is an "On-Demand" hot water heater that, unlike most U.S. water heaters, does not have a storage tank of hot water, but instead only heats the water when it is needed.